KT-523-608

B48 767 990 0

ANIMAL STORY

POLAR BEAR
IN THE CITY

by Dougal Dixon

With thanks to our consultant:

Downs Matthews, Director Emeritus, Polar Bears International

ticktock MEDIA

ANIMAL STORY

POLAR BEAR
IN THE CITY

ROTHERHAM LIBRARY &
INFORMATION SERVICES

J 599 . 78

B48 7679 900

R00055098

Copyright © ticktock Entertainment Ltd 2004
First published in Great Britain in 2004 by ticktock Media Ltd.,
Unit 2, Orchard Business Centre, North Farm Road, Tunbridge Wells, Kent, TN2 3XF
We would like to thank: Jean Coppendale and Elizabeth Wiggans.
ISBN 1 86007 526 6 pbk
Printed in China
A CIP catalogue record for this book is available from the British Library.
All rights reserved. No part of this publication may be reproduced, copied, stored in a retrieval
system, or transmitted in any form or by any means electronic, mechanical, photocopying,
recording or otherwise without prior written permission of the copyright owner.

CONTENTS

THALIE THE POLAR BEAR IS BORN

Thalie's world is a safe, warm, white bubble, about a metre high and two metres long. She shares this cosy den with her mother and her twin brother Mari.

The little family is separated from the winter darkness and biting cold by two metres of snow, with only a narrow breathing hole leading to the outside world.

Thalie is four weeks old and her eyes have just opened for the first time. It will be another two or three weeks before she is able to stand up and walk around in the den, but she is growing fast, fed by her mother's milk.

When Thalie and Mari were born, they each weighed only 500 grams. Amazing, when their mother weighs close to 300 kilograms and is the biggest, land-living predator on Earth.

It is early April. Thalie and Mari are now three months old, and it is time for the family to leave the den.

First, their mother digs through the snow blocking the den's entrance tunnel. Then she checks for danger – wolves or hungry male polar bears who may kill her cubs for food. When she is sure that it is safe, she leads her cubs out into the bright, spring day.

The bears live in the Arctic circle, which is the region at the very top of the Earth. Icy land surrounds the Arctic Ocean, where a large area of the sea is permanently frozen. This frozen area is known as the 'ice cap'. In winter, the ice cap spreads and pushes up against the edges of the land.

During the short Arctic summer, some of the ice on land thaws and plants burst into life. But in winter, the ground is bare. In the Arctic, most life is found in the sea.

The cold waters are home to squid, fish, whales and seals. In some places the changing currents break up the sea ice. This is ideal for the seals because they need to leave the water from time to time. It also helps the polar bears, because when the seals leave the water, the bears can hunt them on the sea ice.

TIME TO LEAVE THE DEN

With their little eyes blinking, Thalie and Mari scramble from the warmth of the den into the fresh, spring air.

Now their mother can stretch herself. Her huge body is ideally adapted for this cold environment. She has two layers of fur: an outer layer of oily guard hairs and a short, woolly undercoat. Her fur looks white, but in fact each strand is transparent. The see-through hairs have a hollow core that scatters and reflects light, making the fur look white. Beneath her fur she has black skin that absorbs heat and a thick layer of blubber that stops the heat from escaping.

Polar bears can get too hot. An overheated polar bear will cool off by gulping a mouthful of snow, having a swim or lying flat to spread its belly on the cold ground. Polar bears spend a lot of their life in the sea. They use their big, broad feet like paddles when they swim. When not in the water, polar bears walk on ice. A covering of fine hair on the soles of their feet keeps the bears from slipping on the ice.

Thalie and Mari's first venture into the open air is a short one, and they soon return to the den. Their hungry mother has had nothing to eat for five or six months and she is keen to hunt. But the family will not travel far from this spot for at least another two weeks.

9

Polar bears are strong swimmers, and today
Thalie and Mari are going to learn this important skill.
The cubs follow their mother from the den, across the snow and
ice, toward the water's edge.

Their mother plunges into the icy waves, but Thalie and Mari are unsure – this is the first time they have seen the sea. The mother bear slips through the icy water. She paddles with her webbed front feet, and uses her hind feet as rudders. Her great, streamlined body leaves hardly a ripple.

She encourages the cubs to join her. Mari jumps in, and, not wanting to be left out, Thalie slides into the waves too. The cubs kick and splutter, but they quickly learn how to move through the water. However, their little bodies are soon tired, and the exhausted babies climb up on to their mother's back. The family swims to the shore. Thalie and Mari's first swimming lesson has been a success.

ARCTIC LIFE

Humans influence all regions of the Earth.

In the last hundred years mining and drilling companies have come to the Arctic looking for oil, gas, valuable metals and diamonds beneath the frozen surface. The mess and pollution that they leave behind can harm the polar bears and their food sources.

At one time many hunters came to the Arctic to hunt and kill polar bears. By the 1970s, hunters had killed so many bears, something had to be done. In 1976, laws were passed limiting the number of bears that hunters could kill, and in some places hunting was completely banned.

The native people who live close to the territory of Thalie and her family are the Inuit. They have lived here for hundreds of years, netting fish, harpooning seals and hunting polar bears. In some places the Inuit are still allowed to hunt the bears, but are strictly limited to an agreed number each year.

Nowadays, outsiders simply come to watch the bears. Special buses with all-weather tyres trundle across the ice, while the tourists take photographs of the animals from the safety of the vehicles.

A year has passed. Thalie and Mari have been eating seal meat since they were weaned at four months old, but they still drink their mother's rich, fatty milk.

Now it is spring again, and the cubs are learning to hunt ringed seals for themselves. This is a good time of year to hunt seals. The inexperienced, young seal pups in a nearby colony have not long been born and cannot swim. The pups are stranded on the ice. Thalie's mother leaves her two youngsters watching and slips silently into the water, heading toward her prey. It is not just the seal pups that are inexperienced, though.

Thalie and Mari are so intent on watching their mother that they do not notice the band of Inuit creeping up behind them with their ropes and harpoons.

Suddenly the hunters attack! The terrified cubs dive into the water, calling for their mother. Thalie scrambles ashore to safety. Her mother swims to meet her, and the two females look back. Mari is trapped – caught by the hunters' ropes and surrounded by dogs. There is nothing Thalie and her mother can do to help him. They will never see Mari again.

THALIE, THE ADULT POLAR BEAR

Thalie is now four years old and has left her mother. Last spring a male bear began to follow the pair of females. Thalie's mother was ready to breed again, and Thalie was chased away by her mother's new mate.

Now Thalie roams the floating ice cap, hunting for herself. She has her own favourite hunting sites and her range stretches for several hundred square kilometres. Thalie's white fur helps to camouflage her against the ice, so she is able to creep up on colonies of beached seals and their pups. She has also learned to find the holes in the ice where the adult seals come up for air.

A patient hunter, Thalie
will wait beside a seal air-hole for up
to four hours. At just the right moment, she leaps. Her great weight crashes through
the ice and, before the seal knows what has happened, it has been dragged out of
the water and killed with a single blow from her massive paw. She quickly eats the
rich, fatty blubber, watched by a pack of Arctic foxes who will wait for her leftovers.

Thalie smells something in the air. Rotting meat – food! She follows the scent for many kilometres along the barren shoreline and finally comes to the source. A dead bowhead whale has been washed up on the ice.

But Thalie is not alone. Polar bears have the best sense of smell in the animal kingdom, and many other bears have been attracted by the smell of the carcass.

Thalie moves in to join the others. They do not fight because there is plenty of meat for everyone. This will probably be their last big meal of the spring. Summer is coming. Soon the sea ice will begin to thaw and break up, making it difficult for the polar bears to hunt for seals among the broken pieces.

Thalie and the other bears will wander inland onto the tundra. Here, the topsoil thaws during the summer while the ground underneath stays permanently frozen. The bears can search for food on the boggy ground. Thalie will eat grass, lichens and berries. The only meat she will find will be nesting birds and their eggs, and small rodents, such as lemmings.

Polar bears are adaptable animals, though. As well as being a predator, Thalie can be a scavenger – and when meat is scarce, even a vegetarian.

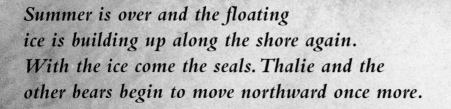

*Summer is over and the floating
ice is building up along the shore again.
With the ice come the seals. Thalie and the
other bears begin to move northward once more.*

Thalie is pregnant. While she was scavenging the whale carcass, she met and mated with a big, male bear. Her pregnancy will last for about eight months, but for the first four months, her baby or babies will not grow. Once winter is under way though, and Thalie has dug a den where she can give birth, the baby or babies will begin to develop. Then they will be born in January. For now, Thalie will need to hunt as much meat as possible so that her reserves of fat will last her through the winter. As she ventures northward, her long, sensitive nose smells something strange and exciting. It is a town, with houses, rubbish tips and restaurants.

POLAR BEAR IN THE CITY

Hungry and curious, Thalie lumbers along the main street of the town. Dogs bark and people hurry indoors!

A polar bear wandering through the town is not a new situation for the people in this region, though. It happens every year, so there is a system in place to deal with it. Although polar bears may mean no harm, their size and strength make them very dangerous animals. A team of specially trained hunters is summoned – a Polar Bear Alert Team.

As Thalie investigates the town dump, the team creep up on her. If they disturb her, she may panic and cause some damage. If they anger her, she may attack in self-defence. The leader of the team loads his rifle and finds himself a good place from which to shoot. Thalie is unaware of the danger. The man raises his rifle – and shoots!

But it is not a bullet that he fires. It is an anaesthetic dart. The people of the town do not want to be harmed by the polar bears, but they also do not want to kill them. Thalie hardly feels the sharp point of the dart penetrating her thick fur and fat. Within a few moments she is feeling sleepy. Then she collapses, unconscious, in the street!

Thalie wakes. She is lying by the sea. She does not know how she arrived here, but she is not troubled. Out at sea there are drifting ice floes, and the water is full of seals — food!

While Thalie was unconscious she was bundled up in a net and lifted from the main street of the town by a helicopter. Her body was carried, dangling and swinging, away to the north and far from humans and their towns.

Every year many bears are moved to safety in this way. Sometimes, while the bears are unconscious, they are fitted with radio collars. The collars send signals, through satellite, to a receiving station where scientists can track the bears to find out where they go.

The team wait for Thalie to regain consciousness. When they are sure that she has suffered no ill effects, they prepare to leave.

As the whirring, rattling helicopter rises, Thalie pays no attention. She is too busy hunting for food.

A NEW BEGINNING

Thalie's world is a safe, warm, white bubble, about a metre high and two metres long. Soon she will share this cosy den with her own cub or cubs.

Thalie is preparing to hibernate. At the first heavy fall of snow, she turned her attention to digging a den. She found a snowy slope on the north side of a hill. If the weather suddenly turns warmer, the snow on this slope will not melt. Then she dug a tunnel and hollowed out a chamber big enough to hold her and her litter.

Thalie's successful hunting has helped her gain nearly 200 kilograms in weight, and her coat has taken on a yellowish colour from the body oils of the seals she has eaten. Thalie will need these fat reserves, because soon her baby or babies will start to grow inside her. Then in January, as she sleeps, her cub or cubs will be born.

Although they were once vulnerable, polar bears no longer face extinction. However, it is only the constant attention of conservation groups that protects them from overhunting and pollution. For now, the future for Thalie and her cubs is secure.

POLAR BEAR FACT FILE

The polar bear's scientific name is Ursus maritimus, meaning 'bear of the sea'.
Polar bears used to be called *Thalarctos maritimus* meaning 'ocean bear of the sea'. In the 1980s, genetic studies showed that the polar bear was so closely related to *Ursus arctos*, the brown bear (or grizzly bear), that it must be a species of *Ursus*. Polar bears are considered to be quite a new species. Scientists believe they evolved from brown bears only about 200,000 to 400,000 years ago.

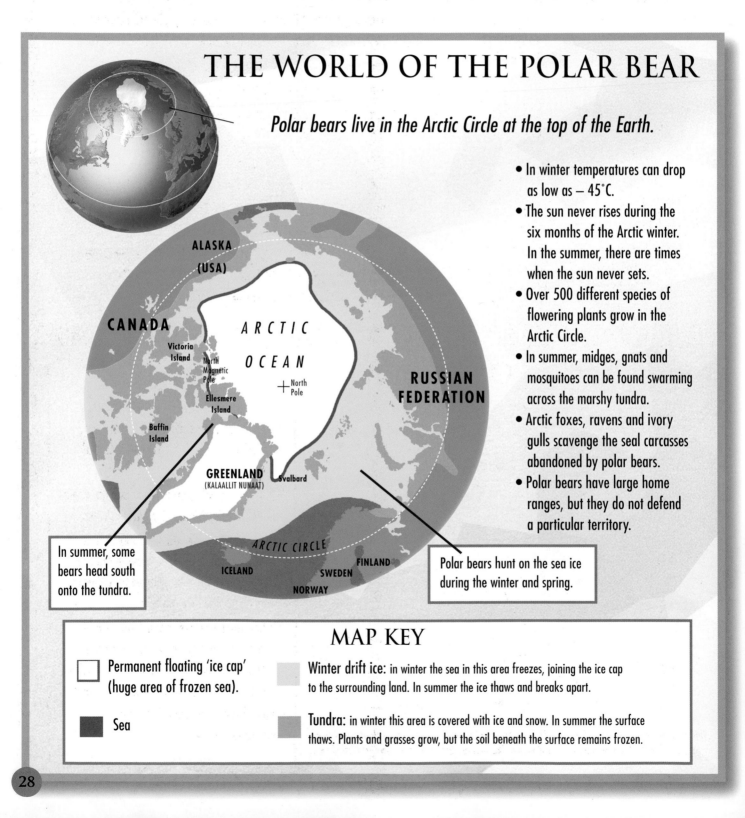

THE WORLD OF THE POLAR BEAR

Polar bears live in the Arctic Circle at the top of the Earth.

- In winter temperatures can drop as low as – 45°C.
- The sun never rises during the six months of the Arctic winter. In the summer, there are times when the sun never sets.
- Over 500 different species of flowering plants grow in the Arctic Circle.
- In summer, midges, gnats and mosquitoes can be found swarming across the marshy tundra.
- Arctic foxes, ravens and ivory gulls scavenge the seal carcasses abandoned by polar bears.
- Polar bears have large home ranges, but they do not defend a particular territory.

ALASKA (USA)

CANADA

Victoria Island

North Magnetic Pole

ARCTIC OCEAN

+ North Pole

Ellesmere Island

Baffin Island

RUSSIAN FEDERATION

GREENLAND (KALAALLIT NUNAAT)

Svalbard

ARCTIC CIRCLE

FINLAND

ICELAND

SWEDEN

NORWAY

In summer, some bears head south onto the tundra.

Polar bears hunt on the sea ice during the winter and spring.

MAP KEY

☐ Permanent floating 'ice cap' (huge area of frozen sea).

■ Sea

Winter drift ice: in winter the sea in this area freezes, joining the ice cap to the surrounding land. In summer the ice thaws and breaks apart.

Tundra: in winter this area is covered with ice and snow. In summer the surface thaws. Plants and grasses grow, but the soil beneath the surface remains frozen.

PHYSICAL CHARACTERISTICS

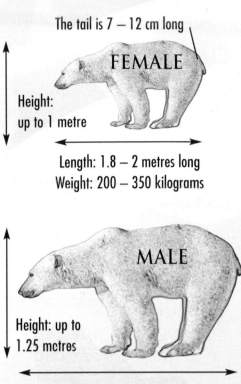

The tail is 7 – 12 cm long

FEMALE

Height: up to 1 metre

Length: 1.8 – 2 metres long
Weight: 200 – 350 kilograms

MALE

Height: up to 1.25 metres

Length: 2 – 3 metres long
Weight: 400 – 600 kilograms

- Polar bears are the biggest, land-living predators on Earth.
- Polar bears can live for 20 to 30 years. However, in the wild, only a few live past 18 years.
- Polar bears have two layers of fur: an outer layer of oily guard hairs and a short, woolly undercoat.
- Polar bear fur looks white, but each strand is actually transparent. A hollow core in the hairs reflects light, making the fur look white.
- The polar bear's black skin absorbs more heat than pale skin.
- Polar bear blubber is approximately 11 centimetres thick.
- Polar bears have small ears and a small nose – this cuts down on the chance of getting frostbite!
- Polar bears have 42 teeth and a bluey-black tongue.
- Polar bear paws measure about 30 centimetres across – the size of a dinner plate! The paws are webbed for swimming and have hair on the soles to help the bears grip the ice.
- Only female bears can wear radio collars (see page 24). Male bears' necks are thicker than their heads, so the collars just fall off!
- A polar bear's body is streamlined for swimming.

ARCTIC FOOD WEB

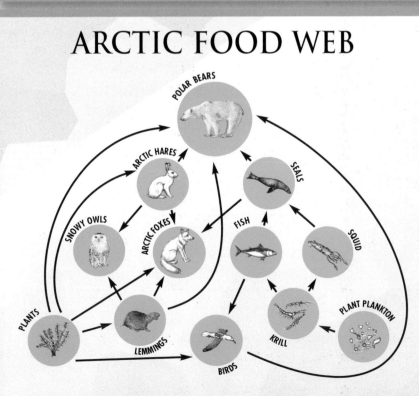

POLAR BEARS

ARCTIC HARES

SEALS

SNOWY OWLS

ARCTIC FOXES

FISH

SQUID

PLANTS

LEMMINGS

BIRDS

KRILL

PLANT PLANKTON

This food web shows how the animals and plants living in the Arctic Circle depend on each other for food – both on land and in the sea. The arrows in the web mean 'give food to'.

DIET

- The polar bear's main food is the ringed seal. They will also hunt harp seals and hooded seals.
- Polar bears will hunt and eat beluga whales, narwhals, dolphins and young walruses.
- Fully grown polar bears eat mainly the seal's rich, fatty blubber, leaving the red meat. This meat is scavenged by younger bears who need the protein.
- When food is scarce, polar bears will eat lemmings, nesting birds and their eggs, berries (such as Arctic bilberries, cranberries and raspberries), grass, moss and lichens.
- Polar bears have even been seen eating seaweed!

CONSERVATION

- Polar bears are the only bears with international protection.
- Scientists estimate that there are 25,000 to 40,000 polar bears in the world.
- In 1976, the US, Canada, Denmark, Russia and Norway passed laws limiting the number of polar bears that hunters could kill. In some cases, the laws ban hunting completely. In some places, Inuit are still allowed to hunt a strictly agreed upon number of bears each year.

- Mining and drilling companies look for oil, gas, diamonds and valuable metals beneath the frozen surface in the Arctic. Conservationists are monitoring the effects that any pollution (chemicals or oil spills for example) is having on the polar bears and their food sources.

BEHAVIOUR AND SENSES

- Polar bears walk at about 5.5 km/h. This slow, but steady, pace stops them from overheating. If charging or fleeing, a polar bear can run at speeds of up to 40 km/h, but only for a very short time.
- Polar bears are so well adapted to the cold, they can get too hot! They cool off by swimming, spreading their bellies on the icy ground, or by eating snow!
- Polar bears are strong swimmers. They can stay underwater for two minutes, and they have been known to swim up to 160 kilometres at a time.

- Only pregnant, female polar bears hibernate. Males, young bears and non-pregnant females spend the winter hunting on the ice.
- Polar bears have the best sense of smell in the animal kingdom – they can smell a potential meal from 32 kilometres away!

REPRODUCTION AND YOUNG

- The polar bear mating season is March to May.
- Pregnant female bears dig out a den on the north side of a slope or hill. They dig an entrance tunnel and a cosy chamber where they spend the winter and give birth to their cubs.

- Cubs are born from January to February.
- New cubs are known as COYS (Cubs of the Year – this year's cubs).
- When they are born, cubs are less than 30 centimetres long and weigh about 500 grams.
- Cubs leave the den when they are about three months old. By this time they are about 40 cms long and weigh about 13 kilograms.
- Mother polar bears wait until spring temperatures reach about 10˚C before taking their cubs outside the den.
- Mother polar bears will carry their cubs on their backs if the babies get too tired.

- Cubs stay with their mother and continue to drink her rich, fatty milk for two to three years.
- Polar bears are attentive mothers. They groom and touch their cubs frequently.

FIND OUT MORE *Polar Bears International: www.polarbearsalive.org*

GLOSSARY

ADAPTED When the bodies of a species of animal have changed, over a very long period in time, so that they are just right for the environment where they live. Polar bear bodies have adapted to suit the cold temperatures in the Arctic.

ANAESTHETIC A drug or gas used to put an animal or person to sleep. It is normally used during operations.

ARCTIC CIRCLE The area in the north that includes the Arctic Ocean and the northernmost parts of Asia, Europe and North America. The area is shown on maps by an imaginary line.

BLUBBER Body fat that mammals (such as polar bears, seals and whales) use for insulation, and as a back-up energy source when food is limited.

CLIMATE The average temperature and weather conditions in a region over a period of years.

CONSERVATION GROUPS Organizations that look after the environment and campaign for the protection of wild animals. Their work can involve many different activities: campaigning against the hunting of endangered animals, cleaning up areas of land or sea that have been polluted and working with governments to get laws passed that will protect the environment.

HARPOON A type of spear with barbs (small points) at the end. Harpoons are sometimes attached to a rope.

ICE CAP The huge area of permanently frozen sea in the Arctic Ocean. The ice in the middle is about 10 metres thick.

ICE FLOE A sheet of floating ice.

LICHEN A plant-like partnership between a fungus and an algae. Lichen can grow on all sorts of bare surfaces, such as rocks or tree trunks.

NATIVE PEOPLES The people who were born and now live in a particular place.

POLLUTION Oils, rubbish or chemicals that have escaped into the air or sea or onto the land. Pollution can damage the environment and harm wild animals and the food that they eat.

SCAVENGER An animal that eats other animals' leftovers or carrion (animals that are already dead).

STREAMLINED When something has a smooth shape and is able to move faster through air or water because there is less resistance.

TUNDRA A boggy landscape of low-growing plants. Below the surface the ground is permanently frozen.

WEANED When a young animal or child begins to eat food other than its mother's milk.

INDEX

A
adaptation 8, 30, 31
anaesthetic 23, 31
Arctic 6, 12, 28
Arctic Circle 6, 28, 31
Arctic food web 29
Arctic foxes 17, 28
Arctic life 6, 12, 28
Arctic Ocean 6, 28

B
behaviour 30
berries 18, 29
birds 18, 28, 29
blubber 8, 17, 29, 31
breeding 16, 20, 30

C
camouflage 16
city 20, 22
climate 28, 31
conservation 12, 23, 27, 30, 31
cubs 4, 6, 11, 14, 20, 27, 30

D
den 4, 6, 20, 27, 30
diamonds 12, 30
diet 29
    see also food
dogs 15
dolphins 29
drilling 12, 30

E
ears 29

F
fat 20, 27
feet 9, 11, 29
fish 6, 12
food 4, 6, 14, 17, 18, 29, 30
fur 8, 16, 27, 29

G
gas 12, 30
grass 18, 29

H
harpoons 12, 15, 31
helicopter 24
hibernate 27, 30
hunting by people 12, 15, 22, 23, 27, 30

by polar bears 6, 9, 14, 16, 17, 24, 29

I
ice 6, 9, 18, 20, 28
ice cap 6, 16, 28, 31
Inuit 12, 15, 30
ivory gulls 28

L
length of life 29
laws against hunting 12, 30
lemmings 18, 29
lichens 18, 29, 31

M
metals 12, 30
mining 12, 30

N
native peoples 12, 31
    see also Inuit
noses 29

O
oil 12, 30
overheating 9, 30

P
physical characteristics 29

plants 6, 18, 28, 29
Polar Bear Alert Team 22, 23, 24
polar bears
    female 4, 16, 20, 27, 29, 39
    male 6, 16, 20, 29, 30
pollution 12, 27, 30, 31
predators 4, 6, 18, 29
pregnancy 20, 27, 30

R
radio collars 24, 29
ravens 28
reproduction 20, 30
    see also breeding; pregnancy
rodents 18

S
scavenging 18, 20, 28, 29, 31
scientists 24
sea ice 6, 18, 28
seals 6, 12, 14, 16, 17, 18, 20, 24, 28, 29

sense of smell 18, 20, 30
skin 8, 29
squid 6
streamlined bodies 11, 29, 31
swimming 9, 11, 29, 30

T
teeth 29
Thalarctos maritimus 28
tongue 29
tourists 12
tundra 18, 28, 31

U
Ursus arctos 28
Ursus maritimus 28

W
walrus 29
weaning 14, 31
weight 4, 27, 29, 30
whales 6, 18, 29
wolves 6

Y
young 4, 30
    see also cubs

PICTURE CREDITS

t=top, b=bottom, c=centre, l=left, r=right, OFC=outside front cover, OBC=outside back cover

Alamy: OFC, 1c, 4-5, 6-7bc, 8tl, 9t, 10-11, 12-13t, 14-15, 16, 20-21, 22-23, 24-25c, 26-27, 30tl, 30b, OBC. Bryan & Cherry Alexander Photography: 13br. Corbis: 6-7 (background), 8-9b, 17, 18-19, 24lc, 24-25 (background), 30tr, 31.

Every effort has been made to trace the copyright holders, and we apologize in advance for any unintentional omissions. We would be pleased to insert the appropriate acknowledgements in any subsequent edition of this publication.